Facts About the Mouse

By Lisa Strattin

© 2019 Lisa Strattin

FREE BOOK

FREE FOR ALL SUBSCRIBERS

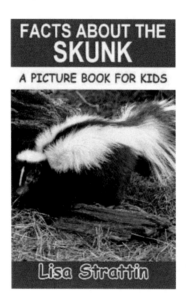

LisaStrattin.com/Subscribe-Here

BOX SET

- **FACTS ABOUT THE POISON DART FROGS**
- **FACTS ABOUT THE THREE TOED SLOTH**
  - **FACTS ABOUT THE RED PANDA**
  - **FACTS ABOUT THE SEAHORSE**
  - **FACTS ABOUT THE PLATYPUS**
  - **FACTS ABOUT THE REINDEER**
  - **FACTS ABOUT THE PANTHER**
- **FACTS ABOUT THE SIBERIAN HUSKY**

LisaStrattin.com/BookBundle

Facts for Kids Picture Books by Lisa Strattin

Little Blue Penguin, Vol 92

Chipmunk, Vol 5

Frilled Lizard, Vol 39

Blue and Gold Macaw, Vol 13

Poison Dart Frogs, Vol 50

Blue Tarantula, Vol 115

African Elephants, Vol 8

Amur Leopard, Vol 89

Sabre Tooth Tiger, Vol 167

Baboon, Vol 174

Sign Up for New Release Emails Here

LisaStrattin.com/subscribe-here

COVER IMAGE

https://flickr.com/photos/14583963@N00/33037462295/

ADDITIONAL IMAGES

https://flickr.com/photos/nick_moise/4285726564/

https://flickr.com/photos/ben124/6223310083/

https://flickr.com/photos/talaakso/2763554556/

https://flickr.com/photos/joe_devereux/25311084779/

https://flickr.com/photos/139753516@N02/51105937580/

https://flickr.com/photos/beyondcoalandgas/9349736368/

https://flickr.com/photos/braydawg/185092747/

https://flickr.com/photos/9750464@N02/49381822727/

https://flickr.com/photos/100915417@N07/49035404616/

https://flickr.com/photos/188355436@N07/50222318318/

Contents

INTRODUCTION

The mouse is a small rodent that is spread widely throughout nearly every country, in all corners of the globe, including parts of Antarctica.

There are nearly 40 different known species of mouse found throughout the world. The different mouse species range in size and color that is generally dependent on their environment.

CHARACTERISTICS

Mice have soft feet with nails on each of their toes that helps the mouse to climb well because they can wrap their feet around things. They have five toes on their two back feet and four toes on their two front feet giving them more stability when standing on their back feet. They use their two front feet to grip onto food like seeds and berries.

Like hamsters, the foot structure of mice enables them to run backwards into their burrows when wanting to escape from predators.

APPEARANCE

Mice can be dusty gray with cream-colored bellies, brown or white. They have four legs and a round-shaped body. Their muzzles are pointed, and their ears are large with some hair.

LIFE STAGES

Once pregnant, the female gives birth after just three weeks. Litters are usually 5 to 8 babies, and the adult females can reproduce up to 10 times per year.

At the beginning of the mouse life cycle, newborns have no hair and are blind. After two weeks, baby mice develop thin fur and slowly gain sight and mobility.

The young mice become adults at around two months of age and are able to reproduce, having their own babies.

LIFE SPAN

The average life span of a mouse kept as a pet is only two to five years. In the wild, they may not even live this long because they are prey for so many animals.

SIZE

Mice grow to be 2 to 6 inches long and only weigh up to 8 ounces.

HABITAT

Mice are hardy creatures that are found in nearly every country and type of terrain. They can live in forests, grasslands and manmade structures easily. Mice typically make a burrow underground if they live out in the wild. Their burrow helps protect them from predators.

DIET

Mice are omnivorous, which means they eat a both vegetation and meat. Pet mice should eat a varied and balanced diet that includes fresh vegetables, protein, store-bought mice food, fresh water and treats.

FRIENDS AND ENEMIES

Mice don't have many friends. People can be their friend in the case of pet mice, but wild mice that move into your house are not your friend.

In the wild, birds, cats, foxes and reptiles will attack and kill mice. As a matter of fact, most animals who eat meat is a mouse predator.

SUITABILITY AS PETS

There are many people who have mice as pets. If you want to have one, be sure to get it from a pet store or breeder who has kept it as a tame mouse from the time it was born. A field mouse, from outside, is not a good choice. Since it isn't used to people, it will probably bite you if you try to handle it or catch it.

COLOR ME

COLOR ME

COLOR ME

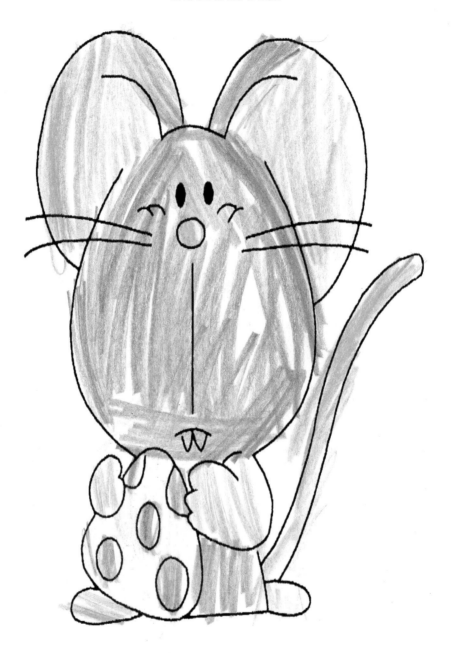

COLOR ME

COLOR ME

Please leave me a review here:

LisaStrattin.com/Review-Vol-209

For more Kindle Downloads Visit Lisa Strattin Author Page on Amazon Author Central

amazon.com/author/lisastrattin

To see upcoming titles, visit my website at LisaStrattin.com– most books available on Kindle!

LisaStrattin.com

FREE BOOK

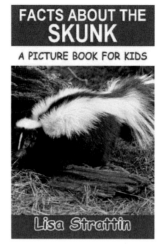

Made in the USA
Coppell, TX
12 October 2023

22767232R00026